Raspberry Pi

The ultimate guide to raspberry pi, including projects, programming tips & tricks, and much more!

Table of Contents

Introduction

Thank you for purchasing this book.

You have no doubt heard about the Raspberry Pi, a palm-sized, cheap and cutting-edge microcomputer that is threatening to make your old bulky PC obsolete. Hackers, hardware geeks and hobbyists cannot stop gushing about the possibilities presented by the Raspberry Pi. But what exactly is it? What can you do with it?

In this book, you are going to learn everything you need to know about the Raspberry Pi and why it is becoming so popular. Some of the topics covered in the book include an introduction to the Raspberry Pi, an overview of the different models of the Raspberry Pi and some of the exciting uses of this amazing device.

You will also learn how to set it up, how to download and install the Raspbian operating system, and how to write your first program for the Raspberry Pi using Python.

What are you waiting for? Let's dive in!

Chapter 1: What Is The Raspberry Pi?

In this chapter, you are going to learn what the Raspberry Pi is and why it was developed.

Computers have come a long way. At the very beginning, they were huge, with a single computer taking up an entire room. As computer technology advanced, smaller microprocessors became available, leading to the manufacture of home PC's like the Commodore 64, the Apple II, and the Tandy TRS-80. Today, computer technology has advanced so much and microprocessors have become smaller and smaller, which has enabled the creation of tiny and powerful computers, such as the Raspberry Pi. If you are a huge fan of computers and tech related stuff, you must have come across the term Raspberry Pi.

What Is The Raspberry Pi?

The Raspberry Pi is a very small and cheap computer. It is as small as a credit card, and you can get one for as low as $5. The most expensive version of the Raspberry Pi costs about $35. However, the Raspberry Pi is not a typical computer like the one you have on your desk. It is simply an electronic circuit board, similar to the one you might find inside your laptop computer. However, it is a lot smaller, measuring about 3x5 inches.

As you can expect from its size and price, the performance of the Raspberry Pi is not comparable to that of your laptop or desktop PC. It is a lot slower and does not come with all the features of a full-sized computer. However, it can still perform most of the functions of a normal computer, and it does this with very low levels of power consumption. What the Raspberry Pi lacks in terms of high-end performance, it more than makes up for with its high level of tinker-ability. With the right skills, you can use the Raspberry Pi to build all kinds of electronics and computing projects.

Essentially, the Raspberry Pi provides you with the raw basics of a computer. These include some RAM, a graphics chip, a processor, USB ports for connecting peripheral devices, an

HDMI port for connecting it to a monitor and an Ethernet port for internet connectivity. The latest version of the Raspberry Pi even comes with integrated Bluetooth and Wi-Fi connectivity. Being a bare-bones version of a computer, you cannot expect to run any advanced software on the Raspberry Pi. However, most versions will comfortably run a Linux operating system. The latest version of the Raspberry even supports a stripped-down IOT version of Windows 10.

Another thing that made the Raspberry Pi so popular among do-it-yourselfers and computer and electronics enthusiasts is that it uses open source hardware. This gives users the permissions to study, modify and redistribute the designs and schematics of the Raspberry Pi. The only thing that is not covered by an open source license is the Broadcomm SoC (System on a Chip), which is the device's primary chip. This SoC controls the main components of the Raspberry Pi, including the CPU, memory and graphics, as well as the external connectivity ports. In addition, many of the projects built by Raspberry Pi users are well documented and distributed under open source licenses, which means that anyone can copy or modify them.

The Raspberry Pi was initially built for education purposes. Its design was inspired by the 1981 BBC Micro. The aim was to come up with a low-cost device that would be used to teach school children some programming skills and to give them a basic understanding of computer hardware. However, owing to its small size, very affordable price, and its versatility, it quickly became a favorite among electronics enthusiasts, tinkerers, and DIY guys who thought it was the perfect device for projects that needed something more than a basic microcontroller. It allows them to build their desired projects while saving them the time and effort of having to build everything from scratch. In recent times, it has also gained popularity as a way for small startups to kick-start their hardware projects.

The Vision Behind The Raspberry Pi

During the early stages of the computing revolution, the computers were nothing like what we have today. While some of the early personal computers came with monitors, most were simply keyboards that you had to attach to your television. They had very small RAM's, and many lacked any internal storage. Many of these early computers did not have any graphical user interface, and for those that had one, it was very rudimentary. This meant that to use the computers, you had to be familiar with some programming. You had to work on command lines and familiarize yourself with the back-end operations of the computer.

During this time, very few software programs were available for purchase. However, there were several books that came with prewritten programs. All you had to do was buy the book and then retype the program's code on your home computer. You could also teach yourself some programming and write your own programs. Whatever you did, you had to have some programming knowledge in order to get the most out of your computer back in those days.

In the 90's, commercial prewritten software started becoming more popular, and computers became more functional for the everyday person. In an attempt to make everything easier, the backend processes of the computer were hidden and replaced by neat and user-friendly GUI's. There was less and less reason for people to access the command line or write their own programs. The result is that nowadays, most people do not know anything about programming. Instead, the focus of using computers has shifted to mundane uses like surfing the internet and sending emails.

The Raspberry Pi was introduced as a way of getting people interested in programming again. It was envisioned as a device that would be used in schools to rekindle children's interest in programming and to teach them basic coding skills. This explains why the Raspberry Pi was built as a low power and low cost device. The idea was that this would make it more readily available in the classroom. The devices immediately gained a lot of popularity after their launch. By March 2018, over 19 million units of the device had been sold.

The name 'Raspberry' was chosen as an homage to early computer companies, most of which derived their names from fruits – companies like Apple, Acorn, Apricot Computers, and

Tangerine Computer Systems. The name 'Pi' was derived from the fact that the device was originally only meant to run the Python programming language.

Chapter Summary

In this chapter, you have learned:

• The Raspberry Pi is a small and cheap device that provides you with the raw basics of a computer, which you can use as a basis for building all kinds of computing and electronics projects.

• The Raspberry Pi was developed with the aim of getting children interested in computing. However, due to its small size, affordability and versatility, it has gained a lot of popularity amongst hobbyists, do-it-yourselfer's, and computing enthusiasts.

Chapter 2: The Different Raspberry Pi Models

In this chapter, you are going to learn about the different Raspberry Pi models and the tasks that each model is best suited for. If you have tried looking at some of the online shops and marketplaces where you can buy the Raspberry Pi, you will already have realized that there are several available models of the device. These different models have different specifications, making each model better for certain kinds of projects. For instance, there is a model that is better suited to projects that have space limitations, while another model is better suited for projects that require wireless connectivity. In this chapter, you will learn about the differences between the main models. This will help you make a better choice when it comes to choosing the best Raspberry Pi for your project.

Before we get down to the different models, it is good to note that there are some components that are standard on all the Raspberry Pi models. For instance, all the models use the same VideoCore IV GPU. All the models also come with a display interface (DSI), a camera interface (CSI) and an HDMI port. However, there is an exception in the Raspberry Pi Zero, which has no DSI connector and comes with a mini-HDMI port instead of the standard HDMI port.

It's also good to note that recent versions of the Pi 2 use the same BCM2837 ARMv8 CPU that is used by the Pi 3. Earlier versions of the Pi 2 used a much slower BCN2836 ARMv7 CPU. The Model A+ also underwent a recent upgrade that saw its RAM increased to 512MB. The upgrade was not accompanied by a change in name or price.

Raspberry Pi 3

This is the latest generation of the Raspberry Pi. The Pi 3 has the highest specifications and is the most powerful version of the Raspberry Pi. It has the most RAM of all Pi's, the fastest clock speeds, as well as the best set of features. This makes it the best option for most general purpose projects. It comes in two models, the Pi 3B and the Pi 3B+. The Pi 3B comes with a 64-bit quad-core ARMv8 CPU with clock speeds of 1.2GHz, 1 GB RAM as well as Bluetooth, WI-FI and Ethernet connectivity. The Pi 3B+, on the other hand, has a 64-bit quad-core ARMv8 CPU with clock speeds of 1.4 GHz. It also comes with faster Ethernet connectivity, Bluetooth 4.2/BLE, dual-band wireless LAN, and supports Power-over-Ethernet. It also has a separate PoE HAT (Hardware Attached on Top) add-on. Both versions of the Pi 3 come with 4 USB 2.0 ports.

The Raspberry Pi 3 is a natural choice when you want speed and power. It is also the best choice when you are working on a project that requires in-built Bluetooth or Wi-Fi connectivity. While the Pi 3 is more expensive than the other models, its price is still fairly affordable, and with its great feature set, it is definitely worth every dime.

With the Raspberry Pi 3, you will get a genuinely pleasant experience that almost compares to what you get from a standard PC. This is largely as a result of the great level of optimization that has been done on the Raspbian – the official Pi operating system – over the years. Unlike what you might expect, the Pi 3 boot process is very fast, and surfing the internet on the device is a breeze. You can even run some pretty intensive applications like Mathematica and LibreOffice and expect almost the same level of response you would get on a decent PC.

The Raspberry Pi 3 is the perfect device when it comes to retro gaming emulation. Its processor is fast enough to reasonably emulate Dreamcast, PSX, and N64. All this for a mere $35. The Pi 3 also runs OpenCV for computer vision a bit more reasonably, something that is an uphill task for previous models like the Pi 1.

The advantages of the Raspberry Pi 3 are its speed and power, as well as its excellent value for money. On the flip side, it requires a lot more power than previous models. The Raspberry PI 3 is best suited for uses like acting as a gaming emulator, a web server, a media center, or a desktop PC. It also works well for computer vision projects.

Raspberry Pi 2B

The Raspberry Pi 2 is the second generation version of the device, the predecessor to the Pi 3. Original versions of the Pi 2 came with a 32-bit quad-core BCM2836 ARMv8 CPU that clocked at 900MHz. However, recent models have been upgraded to the BCM2837 ARMv8 processor that is used by the Pi 3. The processor on the Pi 2 however, has been under-clocked at 900MHz. Like the Pi 3B, the Pi 2 comes with 1 GB of RAM, 4 USB 2.0 ports, and Ethernet connectivity. The only major difference between the Pi 2 and the Pi 3B is the lower clock speed and the lack of Bluetooth and Wi-Fi connectivity.

The Raspberry Pi 2 can be reasonably used as a desktop PC, though it is a little less powerful than the Pi 3. However, considering that both share the same GPU and RAM, you can expect it to handle things almost as well as the Pi 3. Ideally, you can use the Pi 2 for projects that don't require in-built wireless connectivity, and the Pi 3 for those that do. As an added advantage, the Pi 2 requires less power than its younger sibling. The Raspberry Pi 2 is best suited for playing videos, gaming emulation, acting as a web server or media center, as well as regular use as a desktop PC. The only downside to the Pi 2 is that it lacks wireless connectivity despite costing roughly the same as the Pi 3.

Raspberry Pi 1 Model B+

The Pi 1 is the first generation of the Raspberry Pi. The Model B+ was released as an upgrade to the original Model B. As part of the upgrade, the B+ came with two extra USB ports, raising the total to four, and the GPIO header on the device was extended from 26 to 40 pins. The Model B+ introduced the HAT specification which has become the standard for add-on boards. The Model B+ also introduced the new form factor that has continued to be used in later models. The Raspberry Pi 1 Model B+ comes with a 32-bit single-core ARMv6 processor with a clock speed of 700MHz and 512MB of RAM. The only available option for connectivity is Ethernet.

The Model B+ will perform most routine tasks fairly well. However, when compared to the Pi 2 and Pi 3, you might notice a slight sluggishness when performing intensive tasks like running the web browser. This is because the Model B+ uses a single-core processor where the others use quad-core processors. It uses the same GPU as the other models, therefore it can effortlessly handle HD videos. This makes it a good option for running a media center. However, you might notice that the menus will also be a bit sluggish compared to the Pi 2 or the Pi 3.

The extension of the GPIO header on the Model B+ to 40 pins allows you to use the device for more electronic projects. It also allows you to tinker around with HATs. You can connect the device to the internet via Ethernet. If you are working on a project that requires wireless connectivity, you can use a USB dongle to add Bluetooth and Wi-Fi capabilities. The new design introduced by the Model B+ got rid of some ugly components and made the layout of the board more visually pleasing.

The processor used on the Raspberry Pi 1 is one of the most stable, and has been used in several million units. This processor is also the most supported SoC in the world. It even received certification for space flight. Already, there is a Model B+ in orbit on the International Space Station.

The advantages of the Raspberry Pi 1 Model B+ include its very affordable price, the stability of its CPU, and the standard form factor. On the flip side, it lacks wireless connectivity and is less powerful and a lot slower than later models. The Raspberry Pi 1 Model B+ is best suited for use as a media center, for International Space Station missions, for use in information displays, as well as for robotics and GPIO projects.

Raspberry Pi 1 Model A+

The Model A+ is a redacted version of the Model B+. Instead of the Ethernet port and the bank of USB ports, the Model A+ only features one USB port. Just like the B+, it comes with a 32-bit single-core ARMv6 processor with a clock speed of 700MHz and 512MB of RAM. The Model A+ has no available options for connectivity. However, at $20, its price is way lower than later models, and provides good value for your money.

The Model A+ is a bit sluggish when used as a regular desktop PC. If you don't mind this, as well as the lack of internet connectivity, you will have no problem with this device. However, it will probably frustrate you if it is your only Pi. Luckily, if you have a Pi 3, you can do your programming on the more powerful device and then deploy the code on the Model A+.

While not as small as the Pi Zero, its size is still fairly small. This is because the device lacks full size HDMI and USB ports. This means that connecting essential peripherals to the Model A+ will be a headache. However, the small size comes in handy when you are working on projects that have space limitations, for instance, building a small robot.

It's good to note that the Model A+ was upgraded to 512MB of RAM only recently. Previous versions came with 256MB RAM. The upgrade to 512MB makes it more tolerable when being used as a regular desktop PC, though it is a far cry from the performance you get with the Pi 2 or Pi 3.

The advantages of the Model A+ include its low price, its stable processor, its small size and light weight, and its standard form factor. Another advantage the Model A+ has over the Pi Zero is that it comes with a DSI, allowing you to use the official touch screen with the A+. The Model A+ also has the lowest power consumption, which makes it the best choice if your project requires a solar or battery powered Pi, or if it requires the Pi to be left running on low power. On the flip side, the A+ has only one USB port, it lacks any connectivity options and is less powerful and a lot slower than other models. The Raspberry Pi Model A+ is best suited for use in wall displays, robotics, and high altitude ballooning.

Raspberry Pi Zero

If you want the lightest, smallest and cheapest Raspberry Pi, you should go for the Pi Zero. It comes fitted with the BCM2835

ARMv6 processor found on the Pi 1. However, on the Pi Zero, the processor has been overclocked to 1GHz. This means that the Pi Zero is faster than the Pi 2. You should keep in mind, however, that the Pi 2 uses a quad-core processor whereas the Pi Zero is a single-core. The Pi Zero comes with 512MB of RAM, which allows it to give a fairly good level of desktop experience. The power consumption on the Pi Zero is quite low, almost similar to that of the Model A+. The Pi Zero also comes with one USB OTG port. Unfortunately, it lacks any options for connectivity. All the same, it is a great choice for embedded projects that do not require wireless connectivity. In case you need wireless connectivity, you can add the capability using a USB Bluetooth or Wireless dongle. Alternatively, you can opt for the Pi Zero W, which comes with wireless LAN, Bluetooth 4.1, and Bluetooth Low Energy (BLE). It is good to note that the Pi Zero is not available for bulk orders, so it might be a challenge if you need several units.

Since it has a camera interface, the Pi Zero is a great choice for projects where size and weight play an important role, such as in high altitude ballooning. However, it is not a great choice for general purpose computing. This is because you will need a USB hub to connect your peripherals and adapters for converting from micro USB and mini HDMI. However, just like with the Model A+, you can write code on a more powerful device and deploy it to the Pi Zero.

The advantages of the Raspberry Pi Zero are its small size and weight and its very low price. The Pi Zero costs a mere $5. However, you might be put off by its unpopulated GPIO header, the lack of wireless connectivity, and its limited availability. The Pi Zero is perfect for projects involving reconnaissance, miniature robotics, and high altitude ballooning.

Compute Module

If you are working on a very serious project, you might consider using the Raspberry Pi Compute Module. This model is better suited for people who are building a product for commercial purposes and who are constrained by space limitations. The Raspberry Pi Computer Module can be used in a wide range of applications, including on things such as box set TVs, digital signage solutions, and media centers.

The compute module is less of a fully-fledged computer compared to the other modules. The idea is that you should build your own IO board and then hook up the compute module to it. The compute module can be connected to up to two displays and two cameras. However, you will need access to the compute module developer kit to get started. The developer kits costs about $150. The compute module on its own goes for about $30.

Some of the advantages of the compute module include the option for extra displays and cameras, the option for extra GPIO pin heads, and the ability to customize the layout of your device. On the flip side, the compute module is intended for advanced users, and also costs a lot more to get started. The compute module is best suited for people who want to mass produce products that need a custom layout.

Chapter Summary

In this chapter, you have learned:

• The Raspberry Pi 3 has the highest specifications of all Raspberry Pi models. It has the best processor and features Bluetooth and Wi-Fi connectivity.

• The Raspberry Pi 2 is almost similar to the Pi 3, though it has a slightly slower processor and lacks wireless connectivity.

• The Raspberry Pi 1 Model B+ is an improvement of the older Pi 1 Model B, with 2 extra USB ports and an extended GPIO header.

• The Raspberry Pi 1 Model A+ is the original version of the Raspberry Pi. It comes with a single USB port and lacks Ethernet connectivity.

• The Raspberry Pi Zero is the smallest, lightest, and cheapest version of the Raspberry Pi. It is ideal for projects where size and weight are a huge consideration.

• The Compute Module is ideal for those working on commercial projects that have space limitations.

Chapter 3: What Can The Raspberry Pi Be Used For?

In this chapter, you are going to learn about some of the most popular projects that users create with the Raspberry Pi.

One of the greatest advantages of the Raspberry Pi is its versatility. This means that there is no limit to the number of things you can do with this minute piece of technology. Its applications are useful in different fields, from building projects for industrial applications, to being used for monitoring various elements in space. At home, you can use the device to do pretty much anything you can achieve with a low powered computer, from working on documents to watching movies and playing basic games. To make it easier for you to understand how useful the Raspberry Pi is, below are some of the common home uses for the device.

Media Center

Setting up the Raspberry Pi as a media center serving multimedia files onto the TV is one of the most popular uses of the device in people's homes, and it's easy to do. In addition, the device comes with a sufficiently powered Graphics Processing Unit (GPU) that will have no trouble rendering HD media onto a big screen television. A good way of setting up the Raspberry Pi as a media center is to install Kodi on the device, thereby allowing you to playback media from a storage device. You can also stream YouTube videos on the device by installing some plugins.

There are several available options when it comes to setting up your Raspberry Pi as a media center. The two most popular ones use LibreELEC and OSMC (Open Source Media Centre), both of which are based on Kodi. While both options are excellent at playing media content, each has their strong points. OSMC has a neater and more appealing user interface. On the other hand, LibreELEC is much lighter, which means that it is less taxing on the Pi's processor.

To get started, simply choose your preferred distribution and install it on your SD card. You can do this directly or install it using NOOBS. These distributions are compatible with any model of the Raspberry Pi. The only difference you might notice when using these distributions on different models of the Raspberry Pi is varying reaction speeds, with the fastest being the Pi 3 owing to its superior processor. This means that if you don't need Wi-Fi connectivity, any model of the Raspberry Pi will work perfectly as a media center.

SHH Gateway

Normally, if you want remote internet access to devices and computers on your home network from outside, you need the ports on these devices to be opened up to allow outside traffic. However, doing this poses a huge security risk. Your home network and devices become prone to unauthorized access, attacks, and all kinds of misuse. A Raspberry Pi can provide you with a way to get around this problem. The solution is to have a Raspberry Pi installed on your network. You can then allow SSH access to the Pi by setting up port forwarding. You can then use this Pi as a secure gateway to access other computers and devices on the network. Most routers will allow you to set up port forwarding.

If you decide to open up your Raspberry Pi to remote internet access, you should exercise caution in order not to put your network at risk. Below are some key considerations you should keep in mind in order to keep your network sufficiently secure.

The first thing you should do is to change your login password. Raspberry Pi's come with the word 'raspberry' as the default password. By changing the password, you deter many would-be attackers. However, this does not keep you protected from brute-force attacks. You can make your Pi gateway more secure by changing your password and adding 2-factor authentication. However, the best way to ensure total security for your Raspberry Pi is to disable 'password authentication' when setting up your SSH configuration. With password authentication disabled, the Pi will only allow access using the SSH key. Therefore, any attempts at guessing your password will simply fail. Some people also suggest that you can make your Pi more secure by switching the SSH port from port 22, which is the default port to something hard to guess. However, this is not very effective, since an attacker can figure out your true port by running a simple Nmap of your IP address.

You should avoid running other software on the Pi acting as an SSH gateway. This prevents you from accidentally exposing other things. If you have to run other software, run it on another device that has not been opened up to outside traffic. Upgrade your packages regularly to ensure that they are up to date, especially the 'open ssh-server' package. This ensures that there are no known security vulnerabilities.

You should install fail2ban or sshblack. These keep your network protected by blacklisting any users that are found to be attempting malicious activities, such as trying a brute-force attack on your SSH password.

With your Raspberry Pi secured and its ports opened up to outside traffic, you can log into your home network from anywhere in the world, provided you have access to the internet. From the Raspberry Pi, you can then access the other devices on the network using their local IP address. You will be required to enter a password for devices that are password protected.

CCTV

Another popular home use for the Raspberry Pi is to set it up as a camera module for capturing still photos and recording video footage. The videos and photos captured are then saved locally, streamed internally, or uploaded to the internet for cloud storage. There are many reasons why you might consider converting your Raspberry Pi into a camera. However, the most common reasons are for baby or pet monitoring, and security purposes.

To use the Raspberry Pi as a CCTV camera, you need to pair it with the Raspberry Pi camera module, which is an excellent accessory. The module is capable of capturing full HD photos and video, is very programmable and comes with several advanced configurations. You can also pair your Raspberry Pi with the Pi infrared camera module for night time photos and video.

If you want your CCTV camera to capture still photos regularly after a given period of time, you can use Python to write a short script to enable this. Alternatively, you can use the Raspistill command line tool to enable the camera module to capture photos. From there, you can then use the Cron tool to schedule the intervals within which you want the photo capturing scripts to run. You can choose to have the photos saved on Dropbox or another cloud storage service, uploaded to a web server or even displayed on a web app.

If you are after internal or external video streaming, that is also quite easy. There are various options for setting up the Raspberry Pi for live video streaming. You can search on various Raspberry Pi forums to find the easiest option for you. Once you are done setting up your Raspberry Pi for web streaming, all you have to do is position it appropriately and use it to keep an eye on things. If you want the ability to remotely control the camera's direction, you can achieve that using servos. If you intend to use your Raspberry Pi outdoors, you will need to enclose it inside a waterproof casing. You will also need a power source for your device. A good way of doing this is to use PoE (Power over Ethernet) cables.

Home Automation And IOT

In the recent past, the world has been hit by a wave of internet-connected devices. Nowhere has this become more popular than within the home. Our door locks have internet access, we can control light bulbs and curtains over Wi-Fi, and microwave ovens are susceptible to attacks by Russian hackers. Connecting every day devices to the internet has proved to be a great way of automating tasks around the home.

Today, there are plenty of devices and services that have made things very easy for us. For instance, you can buy the Nest thermostat and control your home's heating through your phone, whether you are at home or back in the office. With the

Philips Hue light bulbs, you can switch off the lights in your kid's room using your phone from the comfort of your bed. While these devices make things easy, a Raspberry Pi can make them even easier. With the Raspberry Pi, you can make these devices even more automated by enabling them to work in response to things such as time, as well as in response to input from sensors. For instance, the Philips Hue on its own will not automatically turn on when you enter the room. However, with a Raspberry Pi and a motion sensor, you can take advantage of the Python API on the Philips Hue to instruct it to turn on when someone enters a room.

Similarly, the Nest Thermostat can be configured to turn on the heating when someone is home. However, if you only want the heat turned on only when there's more than one person at home, your Nest cannot do that. However, if you connect your Nest to a Raspberry Pi, you can write up some Python code to constantly monitor the number of phones on the home network, and if there is more than one, it then instructs the Nest to turn on the heat.

You can get a lot more out of your home automation devices by pairing them up with a Raspberry Pi. Similarly, you can achieve a lot without having to integrate the Raspberry Pi with existing IoT devices. You can come up with an automated door opener, an automated backup server, a homemade burglar alarm, or whatever else you want. You are only limited by your imagination.

Tor Proxy And Ad Blocker

People who like browsing the internet anonymously have found another use for the Raspberry Pi. There are several tutorials that explain the process of setting up your Pi to enable you to browse the internet without the risk of surveillance. You can also use a Raspberry Pi to intercept all web traffic within your network and filter out advertisements. To do this, all you need to do is to install Pi-hole software on your Raspberry Pi. This will give you a total ad-free browsing experience on all the devices that are connected to your network.

Desktop PC

Using the Raspberry Pi as a desktop PC is the simplest thing you can do with the device. All you need to start using your Raspberry Pi as a desktop PC is to load an operating system on to the SD card, connect the Pi to a TV or monitor, connect a USB mouse and keyboard, power on your Pi and you are ready to go. If you need internet access, you can use the device's built in Wi-Fi (for the Pi 3 and Pi Zero W), or use the Ethernet port for previous models. The Raspbian operating system – the Raspberry Pi's official operating system – comes with all the tools you need to use your Pi as a desktop PC. If you need any other tools, you can download them through the browser or install them through repositories.

Wireless Print Server

If you have a printer that lacks options for wireless connectivity, you can use a Raspberry Pi to wirelessly connect the printer to your home network. All you need to do is to install a print server on your Pi and ensure it is connected to your home network.

To do this, install the Samba file sharing software on the Raspberry Pi followed by the Common UNIX Printing System (CUPS). CUPS provides an administration console for your printer as well as the necessary printer drivers. You should then configure the Raspberry Pi to ensure that the printer can be accessed by all the devices on your home network. However, to be able to do this, your printer needs to have USB connectivity.

Chapter Summary

In this chapter, you have learned:

• Setting up the Raspberry Pi as a media center serving multimedia files onto the TV is one of the most popular uses of the device is people's homes.

• You can use the Raspberry Pi as an SHH gateway for remotely accessing devices within your home network.

• Using the Raspberry Pi as a CCTV camera is another popular use for the device.

• The Raspberry Pi is a great device for home automation and IOT projects.

• You can use the Raspberry Pi to block ads on your network and to surf the internet anonymously.

• The simplest thing you can do with the Raspberry Pi is to use it as a desktop PC.

• You can also use the Raspberry Pi as a wireless print server.

Chapter 4: Getting Started With The Raspberry Pi

In this chapter, you will learn how to set up your Raspberry Pi. One you have purchased your Raspberry Pi, you might be wondering how you should power on your device and start using it. After all, the device has no power button, no display, no input devices, and so on. This can make the Raspberry Pi very confusing, especially if you are a non-techie. So, what do you need and how do you go about setting up your new device?

Hardware: What Do You Need?

If you intend to use your Raspberry Pi for every day uses, then you will need some input and output devices, as well as a source of power. In particular, you will need the following:

• A micro USB power cable

• A USB keyboard

• A USB mouse

• A micro SD card

• A HDMI cable

• A TV or monitor

If your monitor does not support HDMI, you will need a VGA-to-HDMI or DVI-to-HDMI adapter. If you are using a Pi 1, you can power it using an ordinary micro USB cable. However, the Pi 2 and Pi 3 are more power hungry. You will need a 2A power supply for the Pi 2 and a 2.5A power supply for the Pi 3. If you want to connect your device to the internet, you will need an Ethernet cable. This is not necessary if you are using a Raspberry Pi 3. Alternatively, you can use a USB dongle to add Bluetooth or Wi-Fi connectivity. You might also need some speakers or headphones. If you are using the Pi 3, you can connect the device to wireless headphones or speakers via

Bluetooth. If you do not have wireless speakers, you can still connect your ordinary speakers or headphones to the device through the 3.5mm headphone jack.

Software: Installing The Operating System

As you might have noticed, the Raspberry Pi does not have any internal memory where it can store the operating system. Instead, the device has been designed to boot from a micro SD card. The operating system is held in the SD card, the same way a hard drive does in a PC. There are several operating systems that have been built for the Raspberry Pi, with most of them being distributions of Linux. However, the Raspberry Pi foundation maintains an operating system known as Raspbian, which is the official operating system for the Pi. Raspbian is based on the Debian operating system. However, it has been tweaked and optimized for the Pi, and comes with a lot of useful software.

For advanced users, the process of installing an image to an SD card is quite easy. However, if you are a beginner, it might be a bit challenging. To make the process easier for beginners, the Raspberry Pi Foundation came up with an installer known as NOOBS, which is an acronym for New Out Of the Box Software. If the process of installing an image to an SD card seems confusing for you, your best choice is to purchase a micro-SD card that comes with NOOBS already pre-installed. It is possible to buy the card together with your Raspberry Pi. Alternatively, you can purchase the pre-installed SD card separately. If you already have a micro SD card and would like to use that instead of purchasing a new pre-installed one, you can still install Raspbian by yourself.

Installing Raspbian With NOOBS

The easiest way to install Raspbian on your micro SD card is to use NOOBS. NOOBS makes the process quite simple, even if you have no prior experience using Linux. Before installing NOOBS on your SD, it's always a good idea to ensure that your SD card is formatted. To format the SD card and install NOOBS, you need a computer that has a built-in SD card reader. Alternatively, you can connect your SD card to the computer using a USB card reader.

To format your SD card, download SD Formatter 4.0 from the SD Association website. This program is available both for Windows and Mac. Run the program and follow the prompts to install the formatter on your PC. Connect your SD card to your PC and note the drive letter allocated to it by the PC. Run the SD formatter, select your SD card's drive letter and click on format. It is good to note that the exFAT file system is automatically used for SD cards that are 64GB or more. Unfortunately, NOOBS is not compatible with the exFAT file system. However, their Raspberry Pi foundation website provides information on how you can force-format your SD using the FAT32 file system, which is compatible with NOOBS.

Once your SD is properly formatted, you can now go ahead and install NOOBS. Head over to the official Raspberry Pi website, find the downloads page and select NOOBS. Choose the 'Download ZIP' option and select the location where you want the file to be saved. Once it has downloaded, extract the contents of the ZIP file and drag and drop them into your formatted SD card. That's it. You are done installing NOOBS on your SD card. You can now go ahead and insert your SD card into the Raspberry Pi.

Installing Raspbian Directly With Etcher

Another easy option of installing Raspbian to your SD card directly is to use a program known as Etcher. This option is much faster, and is a great choice when you want to install Raspbian on multiple SD cards. To get started, visit the official Raspberry Pi website on your computer, with your SD card already connected to your computer. Find the downloads page, select Raspbian and choose the 'Download ZIP' option and select the location where you want the file to be saved. Once it has downloaded, extract the contents of the ZIP file. Head over to the Etcher website and download the Etcher program. Open the file and follow the prompts to install the utility on your PC.

Run the Etcher program and navigate to the location with the unzipped files. Select the Raspbian image and then select the drive name allocated to the SD card. In most cases, you will notice that Etcher will automatically select the SD card drive. Click on the 'Burn' button. This will install Raspbian on your SD card. Once it completes the burning process, Etcher will automatically eject the SD card. You can remove the SD card and insert it into the Raspberry Pi.

Powering Up

Now that you have the operating system installed on your SD card, it is time to power up your Raspberry Pi for the first time. Start by inserting the SD card into the correct slot on the Raspberry Pi. Next, connect the mouse and keyboard into the USB ports. Connect the Raspberry Pi to the TV or monitor using the HDMI cable. Ensure that the TV or monitor is already switched on and that the right input (HDMI) is selected. If you intend to access the internet from the Raspberry Pi, plug in an Ethernet cable into the Ethernet port. Alternatively, if you are using the Pi 2 or below, you can connect a USB Wi-Fi dongle for wireless internet connectivity.

Once everything is properly connected, plug in the power supply to boot up your Raspberry Pi. If it is the first time you are booting into NOOBS, you will be provided with a menu. Select Raspbian and give it some time for the installer to install Raspbian. If you installed Raspbian using Etcher, you are ready to go, and therefore your Pi will boot directly to Raspbian's PIXEL desktop environment.

The Raspbian PIXEL desktop environment is similar to what you might have used before on an ordinary desktop PC. Anyone can use the Raspbian OS, regardless of whether you are used to using Mac, Windows, Chrome OS, or Linux. On the top bar, you will find a menu which you can use to access the available programs. Raspbian is a great operating system that comes with a number of applications, including an office suite (LibreOffice), a web browser (Chromium), general utilities (Leafpad text editor, Terminal and Archiver), some games (Minecraft and

Python Games), and some programming environments (Mathematica, Java, Sonic Pi, Python and Scratch).

Apart from the selection of programs that come pre-installed with Raspbian, you can also install a ton of other third-party programs which have been developed for the Raspberry Pi. To install additional software on the Raspberry Pi, you need to be familiar with installing applications on Linux, particularly Ubuntu or Debian.

Adding Storage To Your Raspberry Pi

Depending on the capacity of the SD card you are using with your device, you might find that the available memory is just too little for you needs. Fortunately, you have several available options for adding more storage to your Raspberry Pi.

The first option is to purchase a larger SD card. There are different sized micro SD cards you can easily find on the market. For a reasonable price, you can get micro SD cards with as much as 128GB, which should be enough for most people. Before purchasing the SD card, check the specifications provided by the manufacturer to ensure that it will work well with a Raspberry Pi.

The other option is to use a USB flash drive. The Raspberry Pi allows you to connect and use a USB flash drive as a secondary storage device. Just like micro SD cards, flash drives come in different sizes. You can get easily get USB flash drives with up to 1TB of space.

Finally, if none of the above options sounds appealing, you can purchase a USB external hard drive. However, it's good to exercise some caution when purchasing an external drive for your Raspberry Pi. Look for external drives that are independently powered. If you go for one that draws power from the host USB port, this will present a problem, since the power requirements of the drive might be more than the Pi can provide. Check the manufacturer specifications to confirm whether the external drive will work well with the Raspberry Pi.

Alternatively, you can look for external drives that have been specifically designed for the Raspberry Pi.

Next Steps

So far, we have looked at how you can set up the Raspberry as a regular desktop PC. However, apart from being an affordable miniature PC, the Raspberry Pi also offers a number of interesting possibilities that you won't get on a regular laptop or desktop PC. These include:

GPIO

The Raspberry Pi comes with a 40 pin GPIO (General Purpose Input output) head. The GPIO head allows you to connect some electrical components to your device, including things like sensors, motors, buzzers and lights. You can then write programs to determine how the Raspberry Pi will interact with and control these components.

Add-Ons

Apart from hooking up electrical components to your Raspberry Pi, you can also connect several add-ons through the HAT's. There is a huge community ecosystem of developers and enthusiasts who are constantly coming up with all manner of add-ons for the Raspberry Pi. You can use these add-ons to expand the functionality of your Raspberry Pi.

IOT

The Internet of Things (IOT) is about giving internet access to ordinary equipment that is normally termed as 'dumb'. Since the Raspberry Pi is small and cheap, programmable, and has internet access capabilities, you can use it to give internet access to ordinary things around your home. This is a very popular use by hobbyists.

Chapter Summary

In this chapter, you have learned:

• To get started with the Raspberry Pi, you need a power cable, a USB keyboard and mouse, a TV or monitor and a micro SD card.

• You can easily install the Raspbian operating system on your Raspberry Pi using NOOBS or Etcher.

• The Raspbian PIXEL desktop environment is similar to what you might have used before on an ordinary desktop PC, which means that anyone can use the Raspberry Pi.

• It is possible to expand your Raspberry Pi's storage using memory cards, USB flash drives or external hard drives.

• The Raspberry Pi provides some exciting possibilities that are not available on regular PCs, such as the GPIO, the ability to hook up add-ons and IOT capabilities.

Chapter 5: Learning How To Code For The Raspberry Pi

In this chapter, you will learn how to program your Raspberry Pi using the Python programming language.

From the very onset, the Raspberry Pi was designed with the aim of helping school children learn how to code. Even the name Pi is derived from the Python programming language. As such, the idea of programming is an integral part of the Raspberry Pi. With the Raspberry Pi's versatility and tinker-ability, programming the device is an essential element of getting the most out it. It is through programming that we can convey commands to the device and instruct it on how it should interact with other devices and components.

Despite not having been around for very long, there are several programming languages that have been modified for use on the Raspberry Pi. Basically, the Raspberry Pi supports any programming language that will compile for the ARMv6 processor. While there is a plethora of languages that can be used to program the Raspberry Pi, two of them are the most common. These are Scratch and Python.

Scratch is an easy to use entry-level programming language that was created at the MIT Media Lab by the Lifelong Kindergarten Group. Scratch was developed as a fun way of teaching young people computational and mathematical concepts. If you are a beginner with little prior experience with programming, Scratch is the best language to start with. With Scratch, you do not have to learn and memorize commands and lines of code. Instead, it makes programming easy by employing a graphical drag and drop interface. Scratch comes preloaded with the Raspbian distribution, therefore you do not have to worry about having to install the language separately.

The second popular programming language for the Raspberry Pi is Python. As I noted earlier, the name Pi was derived from the Python programing language, and as such, Python is the official programming language recommended by the Raspberry Pi Foundation. Python is a popular and very useful language that has been around for almost three decades. Learning how to code in Python is also generally easy compared to other programming languages like C, which makes it a good choice for beginners. Just like Scratch, Python comes preloaded on the Raspbian distribution.

Owing to its graphical environment, Scratch is a lot easier to learn than Python. However, Scratch has its limitations, which makes Python the more preferable language for most of the things you are going to be doing with your Raspberry Pi. As such, this book is going to focus on Python.

The Raspbian distribution comes preloaded with a Python development environment known as IDLE where you can input commands. IDLE comes with its own in-built text editor. To make programming easier, the inbuilt text editor is equipped with automatic placing of indents as well as a color-coded syntax. There is also a 'help()' command that is quite useful whenever you need some help with your syntax.

It is good to note that since Python is a text based programming language, you can write Python programs using any text editor. For instance, you can use the Leafpad text editor that comes preinstalled in Raspbian. Another popular choice for Python programmers is a program known as Geany, which also comes preinstalled in Raspbian. When writing a Python program outside the Python IDLE or Geany, do not use word processors such as LibreOffice Writer. Word processors mess up the formatting, which means that your new program will not work properly.

To get started, pull up the Pi menu from the top bar and select 'Programming', then click on 'Python 3' from the dropdown menu. This will bring up the IDLE command line. To bring up the IDLE text editor, click on 'File' and then select 'New'. This will create a new black document on the IDLE text editor. On the first line, write the following code:

```
#!/usr/bin/python
```

This line, usually known as a 'shebang', tells the system that this file should be run using the Python program, which is located in the folder /usr/bin/. This line is the first thing you should add whenever you are writing a program using Python.

In the world of computing and programming, it has always been the tradition to create a program that outputs the words "Hello World!". I am not going to break the tradition, so this is the first program we are going to create on your new Raspberry Pi. Skip a line and then on the third line (this is not a requirement, but it makes your code neater), type the following:

```
Print "Hello World!"
```

Go to 'File', select 'Save As' and name the file 'hello.py' (without the quotes). Congratulations! You just wrote your first Python program on your Raspberry Pi.

Before you can run your newly created program, you will have to open a terminal and navigate to the location where your file was saved. To let the system know that the file is executable, you will need to type the following command:

```
$ chmod a+x hello.py
```

To run your program, type the following command:

```
$ ./hello.py
```

You will see the words "Hello World!" on your screen. That shows that you have successfully created your first program. However, this is a very simple program that is not really useful.

To make the program a little more useful, we'll add some user input. To add user input in Python, we have to create a variable. This is what will hold the information typed by the user. Go back to the IDLE text editor and delete the line with the words "Hello World!" Do not delete the shebang. Now type the following:

```python
name = raw_input('what is your name? ')
```

By adding the above line, you have created a variable (the user's name) and a prompt that will be displayed on the screen (What is your name?). The line also instructs your program to store whatever information the user will type after the prompt. By enclosing the prompt in inverted commas, you are telling the program that the prompt is a single block of text. Using the variable, it now becomes possible to personalize the print statement. To do this, type the following line:

```python
print 'Hello', name
```

The commands are run in order, therefore the print line should come after the line with the variable. If you were to create the print line before the variable line, your program would return an error since it is trying to use a variable that is has not created yet. Save the program and then run it by entering the following at the command line:

```
./hello.py
```

When you run the program, it will prompt the user to enter their name by displaying: "What is your name?" Once the user types their name, for instance 'Mike', the program will display "Hello Mike".

31

Decisions

While adding the variable has added some functionality to our little program, it still doesn't do much. It simply executes the two steps and that's all. To make the program more functional, we will add a decision step that requires the program to look at the input and perform different actions depending on the kind of input it finds. To do this, we will use something known as an 'If block'. An If block basically looks like this:

```
if :

code block
```

The if command will be followed by a value that can be true or false. In our program, we will check that the input entered by the user is equal to a particular value. Add the following code in your program:

```
if name == 'Mike' :
```

Computers don't handle ambiguity well, which is why we are using "==". In programming, each symbol or word used should have one assigned meaning to avoid confusion. The "=" symbol is used for assigning value to variables. Therefore, it cannot be used to check equality, so we have to use "==". By enclosing the term Mike in inverted commas, we are telling the program that it is a block of text. Finally, the colon tells the program that the expression is complete and what is about to follow is the desired action.

Sometimes, it might be necessary for the If command to execute more than a single line of code. This means that we need a way of grouping these lines of code into blocks. Indents are used to achieve this in Python. To insert an indent, you can use a tab or a space. Whatever you choose to use, make sure that you continue using it throughout the entire project, else things will get very confusing, and your program might not work properly.

Now, we need to tell the program what we want it to do "if name == 'Mike'. We will make our little program greet Mike appropriately by entering the following line:

If name == 'Mike' :

print "Mike, you're a great man."

Note that this time round we are using double speech marks instead of the single speech marks. This is to avoid confusion since the text being enclosed contains an apostrophe. To avoid being rude to people who are not named Mike, we need to add an 'else' block that will execute in case the 'if' expression is false. Do this by typing the following:

else :

print 'Hello', name

Finally, we will add a loop to our program. The loop feature tells the programming to keep running until we stop it. To do this, we need to use something known as a while loop, which basically looks like this:

while :

code block

We will instruct our program to stop by entering the word stop. In this case, our while loop will look like this:

```python
while name != 'stop' :
```

In programming, exclamation marks are usually used to mean 'not'. However, this presents a problem for us. If we place our while loop before the 'name = raw_input' line, our program will return an error, since it does not know the value of 'name'. If we place it after this line, it will request for the name once and then go on an infinite loop. To solve this problem, we will assign an empty string to name before our while loop. This prevents the error and ensures that the while expression is triggered. Our program will now look something like this:

```python
#!/usr/bin/python


name = ''


while name != 'stop' :

name = raw_input('What is your name? ')


if name == 'Mike' :

print "Mike, you're a great man"

else :

print 'Hello', name
```

Save your program as hello.py. Like before, you can run it by entering the following at the command line:

```
./hello.py
```

If you have followed the step by step tutorial in this chapter, you will have created your first Python program on your Raspberry Pi. While this is still a simple program, it has given you some introduction to using Python. Since Python is one of the most popular programming languages, there is no shortage of resources which will help you learn the language extensively. Once you are well versed with the language, you will be able to program your Raspberry Pi to do very many things. Like I mentioned earlier, the only limitation is your imagination.

Chapter Summary

In this chapter, you have learned:

• There are several programming languages that can be used on the Raspberry Pi, though the most common are Python and Scratch.

• How to write your first program using Python.

Conclusion

Thank you for taking the time to read this book.

By now, you should have a pretty good understanding of the Raspberry Pi. You know what it is, why it was invented, the differences between the different Raspberry Pi models, how to configure it and some of the applications that you can use it for. You have also learned how to write your first program on the Raspberry Pi using Python.

I hope that this book has shown you the limitless world of possibilities that the Raspberry Pi presents. If, at any time while reading this book, you have grinned to yourself imagining all the interesting projects you can build using your Raspberry Pi, then I have done my job. After all, the Raspberry Pi was made to encourage people to be creative and to explore the wide range of things they can achieve with the device. Even if you decide not to go any further on your Raspberry Pi journey, at least you have a pretty good idea of what this craze is all about. However, there is a high chance that learning about the Raspberry Pi has awakened your creativity engines.

So, what next?

There are no limits to the path you can take to continue exploring the Raspberry Pi. It all depends on your interests. There are lots of forums where people share the projects they have built using the Raspberry Pi, complete with the schematics and working diagrams. All you need to do is to find a project you like and try to replicate it on your Raspberry Pi. You can start by trying small projects, such as setting up your Raspberry Pi as an ad blocker, a media center, or to automate some tasks at home. You might also decide to use the Raspberry Pi to improve your Linux command line skills or your programming skills. As you get better with the device, you will find yourself working on more and more complex projects.

The Raspberry Pi will become a great tool for experimenting and expressing your creativity. Keep practicing, and you will be able to work on any projects you can think of. There is also a very large Raspberry Pi community, which means that there is no shortage of resources that you can use to improve your skills.

Finally, I would really appreciate it if you take a minute to leave an honest review about this book.

All the best as you embark on your journey with the Raspberry Pi.